Collins

easy l

Shapes, colours and patterns

Ages 3–5

Carol Medcalf

How to use this book

- Find a quiet, comfortable place to work, away from distractions.

- This book has been written in a logical order, so start at the first page and work your way through.

- Help with reading the instructions where necessary and ensure that your child understands what to do.

- This book is a gentle introduction to shapes, colours and patterns. Try to use the following language as you work through the book together: sides, corners, points, edges, colour names, shape names, pattern, same, different.

- If an activity is too difficult for your child then do more of our suggested practical activities (see Activity note) and return to the page when you know that they're likely to achieve it.

- Always end each activity before your child gets tired so they will be eager to return next time.

- Help and encourage your child to check their own answers as they complete each activity.

- Let your child return to their favourite pages once they have been completed. Talk about the activities they enjoyed and what they have learnt.

Special features of this book:

- **Activity note:** situated at the bottom of every left-hand page, this suggests further activities and encourages discussion about what your child has learnt.

- **Shapes, colours and patterns panel:** situated at the bottom of every right-hand page, this shows the shapes, colours and patterns that have been covered. Use this to recap what your child has learnt.

- **Labelled pictures:** these should be used to introduce the colour or shape. Spend time using the pictures to discuss things that are red and blue, for example.

- **Certificate:** the certificate on page 24 should be used to reward your child for their effort and achievement. Remember to give them plenty of praise and encouragement, regardless of how they do.

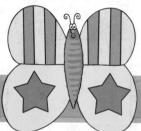

Published by Collins
An imprint of HarperCollins*Publishers* Ltd
The News Building
1 London Bridge Street
London
SE1 9GF

Browse the complete Collins catalogue at
www.collins.co.uk

© HarperCollins*Publishers* Ltd 2006
This edition © HarperCollins*Publishers* Ltd 2015

10 9 8 7 6 5

Printed and bound in Great Britain by Bell and Bain Ltd, Glasgow

ISBN 978-0-00-815157-7

The author asserts the moral right to be identified as the author of this work.

British Library Cataloguing in Publication Data

A Catalogue record for this publication is available from the British Library.

Written by Carol Medcalf
Design and layout by Lodestone Publishing Limited and Contentra Technologies Ltd
Illustrated by Jenny Tulip
Cover design by Sarah Duxbury and Paul Oates
Project managed by Sonia Dawkins

MIX
Paper from responsible sources
FSC™ C007454

Contents

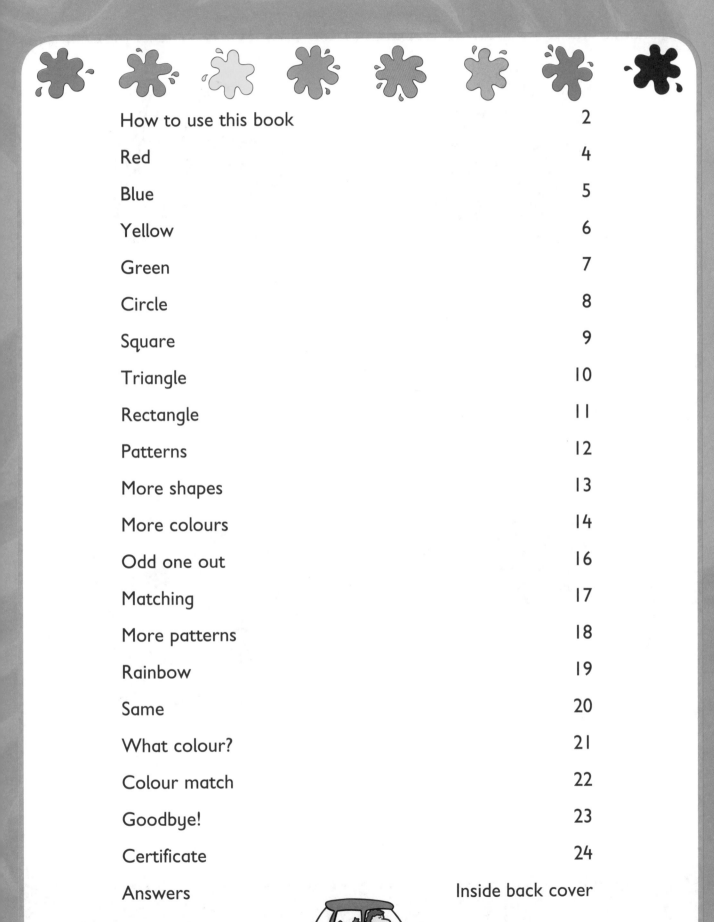

Red

red

● Colour the pictures red.

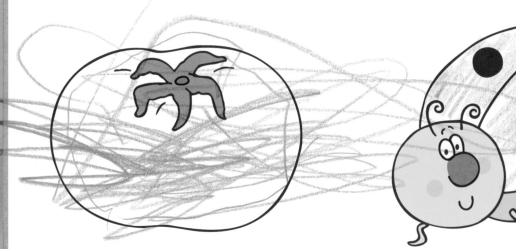 

Encourage your child to think of other things that are red and blue. Play the 'I spy' game. Say: 'I spy with my little eye, something that is the colour…red.' Your child needs to guess what it is.

Blue

blue

● Colour the pictures blue.

Yellow

yellow

● **Colour the pictures** yellow.

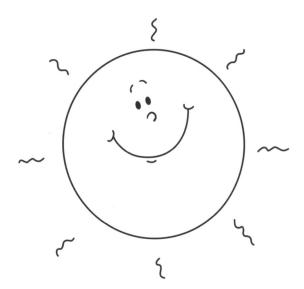 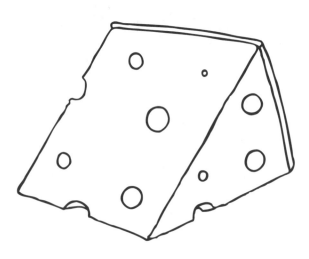

Take coloured sheets of paper outside (different shades of red, blue, yellow and green). Match things that you find outside to the sheets of paper, and talk about the variety and shades of colours.

Green

green

● Colour the pictures green.

Circle

● Trace the circle. Draw your own.

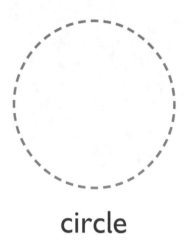

circle

● Find the circles in the picture. Colour them red.

Try to find as many shapes as you can in the place that you're in. Count them all. Which shape can you find the most of? Which shapes are difficult to find?

Square

- Trace the square. Draw your own.

square

- Join the dots to make squares. Colour them blue.

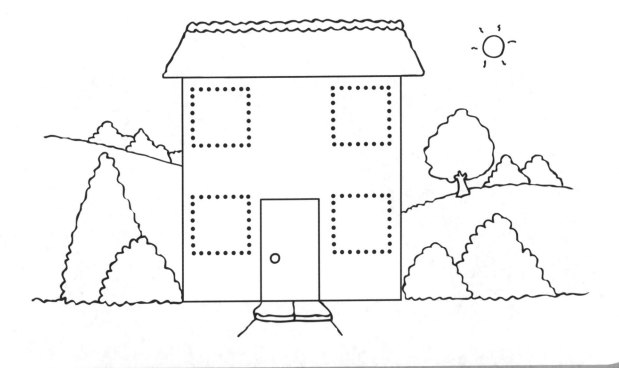

Triangle

- Trace the triangle. Draw your own.

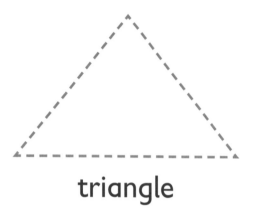

triangle

- Find the triangles in the picture. Colour them yellow.

Cut shapes out of paper and make a shape picture together. Look at the shapes and discuss them (size, colour, number of sides, etc). Fold squares in half diagonally – what have you got? A triangle!

Rectangle

- Trace the rectangle. Draw your own.

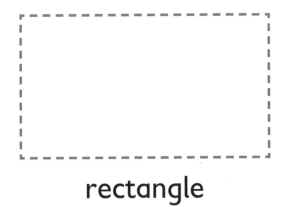

rectangle

- Join the dots to make rectangles. Colour them green.

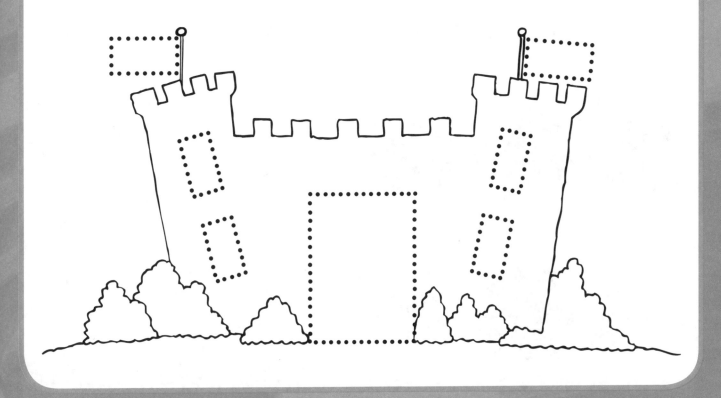

Patterns

- Draw the next two shapes to finish the pattern.

- Colour the next three to finish the pattern.

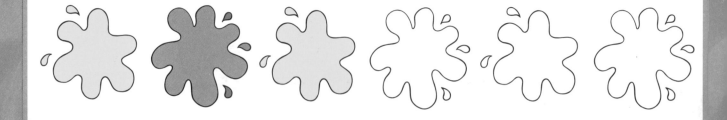

Look at patterns on clothes, windows, paving, etc. See what you can find, and discuss the patterns and regularity.

More shapes

- Trace the shapes. Draw your own.

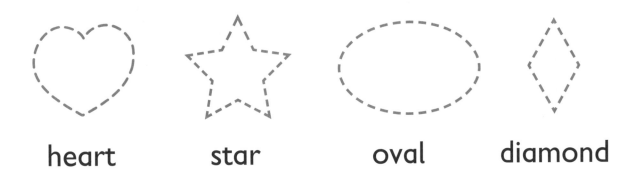

heart   star   oval   diamond

- Find the shapes in the picture below. Colour them.

♡ = red   ☆ = yellow   ◯ = blue   ◇ = green

More colours

pink

orange

- What colour is a flamingo? What colour is a fish? Choose pink or orange and colour the pictures.

purple

black

● What colour are grapes? What colour is a bat? Choose purple or black and colour the pictures.

Odd one out

Cross the odd one out in each row.

Look at each shape together. Talk about how many edges and corners each one has. This will help your child to familiarise themselves with different shapes and be able to identify them easily.

Matching

Draw lines to match the shapes.

More patterns

- Colour the right wing on each butterfly to match the colour pattern on the left wing.

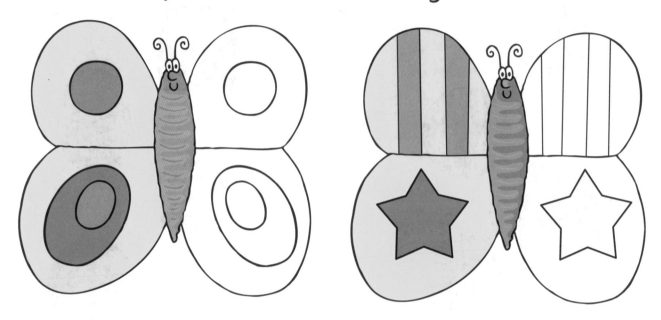

- Draw a line to match the eggs to the correct eggcups. Look carefully at the patterns.

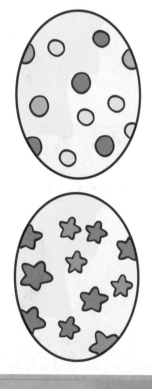

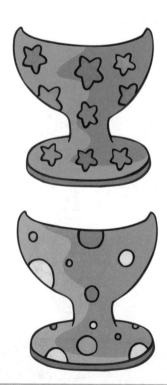

Play noughts and crosses. As well as teaching shapes and pencil control, children learn to think ahead and learn about patterns.

Rainbow

- Use the colour key to colour the rainbow.

  r = red   o = orange   y = yellow

  g = green   b = blue   p = purple

Same

Look at the first picture in each row. Draw a circle round the picture that is the same.

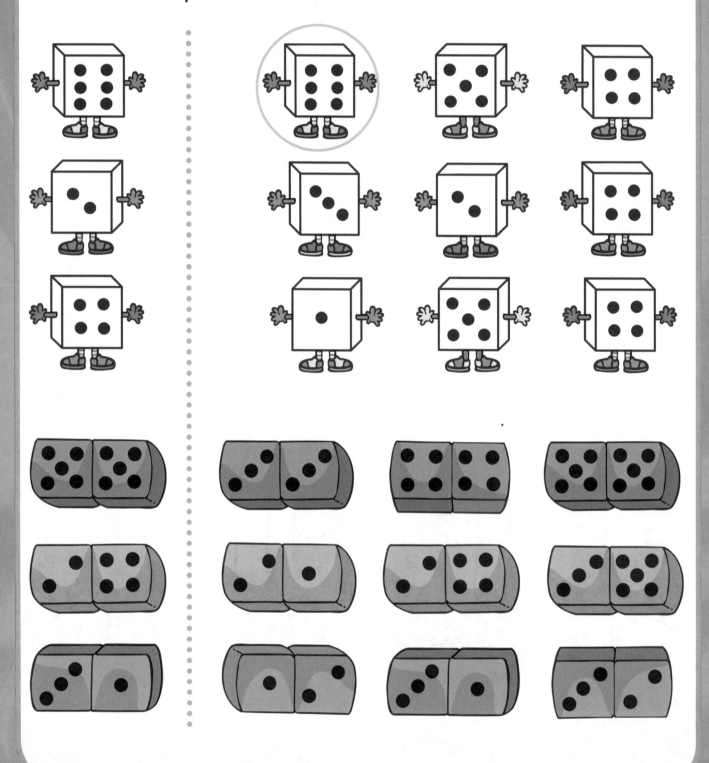

Play dominos or games with dice, this is a great way of getting children to read patterns and is a gradual introduction to numbers.

What colour?

- Draw lines to match each fruit to the correct colour word. Colour the fruit that colour.

yellow

red

green

purple

orange

Colour match

● Join the dots to make shape kites. Colour the kite to match the child's T-shirt. Say the colour and shape of each kite.

Reinforce recognition of shapes and colours by asking your child to find a specific coloured shape. Use the activity on page 23 to start, and then ask them to find other shapes around the room/place you are in.

Goodbye!

- What shapes can you find in the picture? Say the name and colour of all the shapes.

Well done .... (name)

You have finished!

Now you know all your shapes and colours!

Date ....

Age ....